AF505413

Success

HOW DOES SUCCESS MATTER TO GOD

How Does Success Matter to God, Copyright ©
2022
by John W. Boland. All rights reserved.

No part of this publication may be reproduced,
stored in a retrieval system or transmitted in any
way by any means, electronic, mechanical,
photocopy, recording or otherwise without the prior
permission of the author except as provided by
USA copyright law.

Scripture quotations, unless otherwise indicated,
are taken from the Holy Bible, King James Version,
Cambridge, 1769. Used by permission. All rights
reserved.

Scripture quotations marked (MSG) are taken from
The Message. Copyright © 1993, 1994, 1995, 1996,
2000, 2001, 2002. Used by permission of NavPress
Publishing group. All rights reserved.

Scripture quotations marked (CJB) are taken from
the Complete Jewish Bible by David H. Stern.
Copyright © 1998. All rights reserved. Used by
permission of Messianic Jewish Publishers, 6120
Day Long Lane, Clarksville, MD 21029.
www.messianicjewish.net.

Published in the United states of America
ISBN: 9798847585958
Imprint: Independently published
1.Nonfiction > Business & Economics > Leadership
2.Nonfiction > Business & Economics >
Organizational Behavior

TABLE OF CONTENTS

INTRODUCTION

Visualize success with me if you can?

- Money, status, or keeping up with the neighbors?
- Climbing the corporate ladder?
- Keeping a journal of all your achievements, accomplishments & honors?
- Being loyal to yourself, family, friends, or organizational goals?
- Being brutally honest?
- Following a work plan?
- Having a strong work ethic?
- Meaningful or fulfilling work?
- Having the love and support of your family?
- Being a trend setter in your industry or profession?
- Building a great company or workplace?
- An internal sense of satisfaction and accomplishment?
- Doing things that you really enjoy?
- Conducting life with integrity and perseverance?
- Gaining material wealth?
- Life without comparison?
- Having a balanced lifestyle?
- Surviving failure?
- Making the world a better place?
- Continuously growing and evolving?
- Bettering yourself?

- Benefitting others?
- Adopting one's attitude, habits, emotions and mindset on a dream and achieving that vision?
- Simply being happy and grateful?
- Having inner peace, self-respect, and pride in what you do?
- Not waiting until retirement to enjoy life?
- Love yourself

PERSONAL WINDOW

A 12-year-old boy received a letter from then Vice President Richard Nixon which thanked him for writing about the need for peace in the world. It was from that experience that developed the dream in that young man of being President of the United States. For years after that experience his studies and focus centered around history and political science. It later showed up as a career in politics in cities and at the state level. He never rose to the national level. He never wanted to put his family through that ugliness. Can it be said that what followed was a successful career? I think so! There were opportunities to manage multiple cities out of depths of unbelievable debt for 8 years. What followed was keeping a college financially sound for 12 years. Then later on came teaching history, political science, and speech at the high school, college, and university levels for 38-years. Were these the first choice? Not according to that 12-year-old boy. However, dreams change, based on the reality of life. For the adult in me success is being positive, doing your best, making a difference, and bringing honor and glory to God in all you do.

So, what is your vision of success? Did any of the statements above match your visualization of success? How do the concepts of success as stated in Scripture differ from that promoted by the secular world? Let's take a look!

WHAT IS SUCCESS

The Secular World View

Too many in the secular world believe that success is based on money, status, and possessions. To those within that world, success is more about a selfish pipe dream defined by one's own potential and personal limitations. To a few others, it is about being truthful, strong in character, and focused on an outcome of what truly matters in life. Then there are those who find it simply means being available to help others. To a few others, it is the simple a sense of accomplishment. The younger generation seem focused on climbing the corporate ladder. Then there are those who might want to have enough time to do something they love. There are definitely those who just want to provide for their family. For many in the secular world success focuses on performing at their best, bringing to life the characteristics "others" admire, or just accomplishing everything they want in life.

Success could mean a willingness to breakthrough life's consistent failures that seem to plague them. Success might even mean attaining personal objectives. Success could be the realization of meeting those long-term goals based on the attainment of short-term rewards.

The idea of long-term success is based on hard work and acquiring those short-term incentives. The idea of hard work has to have the sense of being rewarded or the dream of success fades. The prize could be the effective use of a person's strengths and skills. The return could be doing something they enjoy and not dreading doing it. The incentive could be a sense of competence in a job well done. The compensation could be doing something long enough to see long-lasting effective results.[i]

Biblical View

Scripture clearly says that prosperity and good success is found in God's Word.[ii] It is not enough for us, to hear, and read God's Word. It is not enough for us, to give lip service or have high regard for it. It is not enough for us, to defend or intelligently discuss it. We must know and remember it. We must put it into practice. We must do according to what was written. We cannot do just what pleases us. We must follow that which is displeasing to our flesh and blood. We must not turn away from it. We must be strong and courageous in following it, even in the face of ridicule, mockery, and discouragement. We must understand that through following the scriptures God will encourage, comfort, and give us success beyond our wildest dreams.[iii] Therefore, according to a biblical world view, success is being in the middle of God's Will both in our personal, family, and work life.

BIBLE STUDY

Joshua 1:8
> This book of the law shall not depart
> out of thy mouth; but thou shalt
> meditate therein day and night, that
> thou mayest observe to do according to
> all that is written therein: for then thou
> shalt make thy way prosperous, and
> then thou shalt have good success.

2 Samuel 23:11-12 (MSG)
> Shammah son of Agee the Hararite was
> the third of the Three. The Philistines
> had mustered for battle at Lehi, where
> there was a field full of lentils. Israel
> fled before the Philistines, but
> Shammah took his stand at the center
> of the field, successfully defended it,
> and routed the Philistines. Another
> great victory for God!

2 Chronicles 26:16 (MSG)
> But then the strength and success went
> to his (King Uzziah's) head. Arrogant
> and proud, he fell. One day,
> contemptuous of God...

Matthew 7:13-14 (MSG)
> Don't look for shortcuts to God. The market is flooded with surefire, easygoing formulas for a successful life that can be practiced in your spare time. Don't fall for that stuff, even though crowds of people do. The way to life, to God, is vigorous and requires total attention.

Proverbs 16:3 (CJB)
> If you entrust all you do to Adonai, your plans will achieve success.

Job 5:12
> He (God) frustrates the schemes of the cunning, so that they achieve no success;

Please answer the following questions:
- What is success according to scripture?
- What is the difference between scriptural and secular success?
- Which are you pursuing and why?

Boland

Success

FAILURE
vs.
SUCCESS

*If you entrust all you do to Adonai,
your plans will achieve success.*
Proverbs 16:3 (CJB)

*Pride goes before destruction,
and arrogance before failure.*
Proverbs 16:18 (CJB)

Quotes on Failing

I have not failed. I've just found 10,000 ways that won't work. Thomas A. Edison

My great concern is not whether you have failed, but whether you are content with your failure.

Abraham Lincoln

Failures, repeated failures, are finger posts on the road to achievement. One fails forward toward success. C. S. Lewis

The greatest glory in living lies not in never falling, but in rising every time we fall.

Ralph Waldo Emerson

I think and think for months and years. Ninety-nine times, the conclusion is false. The hundredth time I am right. Albert Einstein

We failed, but in the good providence of God apparent failure often proves a blessing.

Robert E. Lee

Socialism is a philosophy of failure, the creed of ignorance, and the gospel of envy, its inherent virtue is the equal sharing of misery.

Winston Churchill

Failure is simply the opportunity to begin again, this time more intelligently.
Henry Ford

Anyone who tries to live by his own effort, independent of God, is doomed to failure.

Galatians 3:10(MSG)

Failure is defined as not achieving a desired end. It is being insufficient or falling short of a goal. It is not performing something correctly.[iv]

FACT:
> *Everyone has or will experience*
> *failure sometime in their life.*
> *How they deal with it matters.*

Some people learn from the experience of failure. Others fall on their professional sword because of it. The most rise above each experience to be more successful in the future. Then there are those who just move on not learning from the experience. It is a natural response to try to avoid anything which could end in failure. The very thought of failing provides embarrassment and brings on pain. But what is failure exactly? The very concept of failure is what we create in our mind. We connect our sense of self-worth, self-esteem, and self-acceptance to the goals we set as achievements, accomplishments, and success. We brush aside any idea that failure might be one possibility in attaining these life goals.

To fail is to believe that you did not achieved a goal. That concept of failure is fairly simple and straightforward. Knowing if you failed is only known by keeping data. However, the truth is that failure is in the eye of the beholder. This could be you, as the individual, who believes you did not attain a personal or professional goal. This could be a boss who asked for a project to be completed by a required date, and it was not. This could be a client or customer who requested something and did not get whatever. It could be you looking back on your life and telling yourself you could have or should have done more. Any of these or in any scenario could be a sense that individuals tried hard to achieve a set goal, performed a requested action, or completed a task and did not quite achieve one's objective. Maybe they gave it every effort and still came up short. The problem could have been time constraints, unreasonable expectations, impossible conditions or any number of circumstances. It is then an opportunity to review, assess, and regroup. It is not a time to blame, accuse, or demean.

When dealing with failure consider the following. If you are new at something, success is less likely. Consider the learning curve. You probably won't be successful on the first try. Don't fear the possibility of failing. As someone experiences failure they don't avoid the prospect they rise to the challenge. They look at ways to avoid it or work around it. Don't look at the chaos unfolding in the world as a marketplace for failure, look at it more as a challenge to succeed. Be open to use every circumstance that unfolds before you as a chance to showcase your strength, innovation, creativity, and talents.

Personal Window

If we are honest with ourselves, we must admit that failure is or will be a lifelong friend. In the profession of city management it is a common practice to be fired. Many professional managers have been asked to leave because of upsetting the local supporters of mayors and city council members. Managers can restore financial stability. They can start projects never thought possible and then be shown the door. However, what appears to be a failure in one city can be seen as positive by another city. When your contract is not renewed by one employer because of your high ethical standards may well be seen as a positive by other employers. It all depends on one's conduct and character as conditions unravel. As time goes on in situations like this eventually it becomes clear concerning one's good reputation. Perhaps you are being transferred from one job to another? It too can be viewed as a failure or success based on how you handle it, your character and conduct. How a person views their situation is also important. Consider the idea of self-assessment. It is important to resolve each situation placed before you with as little collateral damage as possible. Also the be aware of the emotions that follow, such as: anxiety, rumors, and self-fulfilling prophecies. The thing you learn as life throws curve balls at you is that God is faithful. God doesn't put you in situations you cannot handle. God provides for you needs and your family. God gives you a way out of each situation if you only believe and look for them.

Success

BIBLE STUDY

Galatians 3:9-10 (MSG)
> So those now who live by faith are blessed along with Abraham, who lived by faith—this is no new doctrine! And that means that anyone who tries to live by his own effort, independent of God, is doomed to failure. Scripture backs this up: "Utterly cursed is every person who fails to carry out every detail written in the Book of the law."

2 Corinthians 13:5 (MSG)
> Test yourselves to make sure you are solid in the faith. Don't drift along taking everything for granted. Give yourselves regular checkups. You need firsthand evidence, not mere hearsay, that Jesus Christ is in you. Test it out. If you fail the test, do something about it.

1 Corinthians 10:13
> There hath no temptation taken you but such as is common to man: but God is faithful, who will not suffer you to be tempted above that ye are able; but will with the temptation also make a way to escape, that ye may be able to bear it.

Please answer the following questions:
- What so the previous verses say about failure?
- What is your thoughts on failure?

Success

MEASURING SUCCESS

Lord, make me to know mine end,
and the measure of my days,
what it is: that I may know how frail I am.

Psalm 39:4

Secular World View

So, how does one determine success? In the secular world, people being interviewed for various jobs are faced with their own idea of success and failure. They must figure out what the interviewers are looking for in their search. The person looking for a job must focus their answers on the successfully addressing the questions. They must figure out how to answer the question correctly in order to attain a new job. Each job is different. Each interview and interviewer is different. The person being interviewed must then focus on the current interviewer in front of them and their idea of who a successful employee looks and sounds like.

So, what is success based on the secular world? Is success the same for a line worker, manager, supervisor, executive, owner? It seems that the secular world thinks success is...

- Meeting the minimum expectations.
- Doing a job correctly.
- Achieving an identity in some way.

- Making money.
- Growing a customer base.
- Being a happy and motivated employee.
- Being self-satisfied.
- Being profitable in business.
- Achieving life milestones.
- Achieving balance in life
- Improving one's knowledge base.
- Developing efficient time management.

So, success then is about quality and quality. It is those things that are measurable on data sheets, financial reports, and the bottom line.[v] Success requires attention to who you are, where you are going, what you are doing, and the results you wish to see.[vi]

Biblical View

So, what does God think of success in business? Well, the book of proverbs has plenty to say about success.[vii] God declares that too be successful one must have complete dependence on Him if they are to succeed.[viii] A person must work hard because that is the opposite of laziness.[ix] Too much sleep will rob an individual of their success.[x] Success is not that easy to achieve, it takes persistence.[xi] A person is to exercise honesty and uprightness in all that they do, because dishonesty offends God.[xii] Dishonesty is bad business whether personal, in the workplace or board room.[xiii] Wise planning of anything you undertake provides long term stability. Always seek the Lord before you begin planning.[xiv] Be meticulous in your dealings, in your outlook on life, and in who you deal with.[xv] Remember do not be unequally yoked in anything you do! Be organized in everything you do.[xvi] Do not co-sign a loan for anyone.[xvii] Always be willing to learn and never be too old to learn.[xviii] In

God's eyes it is not about wealth or material gain. Be cautious of the attraction of wealth and material possessions.[xix] Since God owns everything, be generous with everything you have. Your financial rewards come from God and He promises that it will lead to financial success.[xx] Give it to God's service and those in need. Don't pass up the opportunity to mentor. Seek opportunities both to mentor and be mentored.[xxi] Be proactive in your life, take advantage of every opportunity put before you. Don't drag your feet when a door opens or a door closes.[xxii] Pay your bills on time, don't overextend your credit, and always pursue excellence.[xxiii] Be happy in the work, profession, career you choose to do![xxiv]

BIBLE STUDY

Joshua 1:8

> This book of the law shall not depart out of thy mouth but thou shalt meditate therein day and night, that thou mayest observe to do according to all that is written therein for then thou shalt make thy way prosperous, and then thou shalt have good success.

1 Samuel 15:22

> Does the LORD take pleasure in burnt offerings and sacrifices as much as he does in obedience? Certainly, obedience is better than sacrifice; paying attention is better than the fat of rams.

Please answer the following question:
- How does God see success from these verses?
- How do you measure success?

Success

ASSESSING SUCCESS

My son if you receive my words and
treasure up my commandments with you,
making your ear attentive to wisdom and
inclining your heart to understanding...
then you will understand the fear of the
Lord and find the knowledge of God.

Proverbs 2:1-2,5-6

Secular World View

No one achieves true success without understanding their value system. They can be working really hard all their life in pursuit of something only to find out that what they are engaged in was not worth pursuing. This then becomes demoralizing.

The secular world would have us measure success by comparing our accomplishments to that of our peers. In other words, if your friend makes more money than you, then you're a failure. If your friend gets promoted and you don't, you're a failure. If your friend gets recognized and you don't, you're a failure. If your friend is married and you aren't, you're a failure. If your friend has many children and you don't, you're a failure. All this is based the idea of social reasoning and intellectual bias. It explains how society influences our judgment and easily influences people to compare ourselves to others. Coach John Wooden focused his measurement of success on something more personal: [xxv]

"Don't measure yourself by what you've accomplished, but rather by what you should have accomplished with your abilities..."

To the secular world success is something very fluid. Consider the following questions:

- What is your personal definition of success?
- What is it that you want to achieve?
- Are you clear on what you want to achieve?
- Why do you want to achieve something specifically?
- Where are you in that picture?
- Structurally, is success a weekly, monthly, yearly, short-term, long-term thing?
- Is your idea of success a "system"[xxvi] or a "mindset"[xxvii]?

To the secular world success isn't measured by a certain age, time, or deadline. It isn't about another person's standard or system of measurement except that of the person measuring. It is said that success must match the "rhythm of a person's soul."[xxviii] The reality is that more often than not when a person compares themselves to others it leaves them feeling dissatisfied and inadequate. Such feelings of inadequacy causes one to lose sight of personal strengths, achievements, and accomplishments. Comparison skews reality and highlights insecurities while exaggerating the achievements, accomplishments, and attainments of those we are focused on.

However, when we understand and pursue things we attach importance to, believe that what we are focused on is worthy of our time and effort we then achieve real success and accomplish much. But how do we really know what to pursue? It's all about where we place our values...

BIBLE STUDY

Joshua 1:8

> This book of the law shall not depart out of thy mouth; but thou shalt meditate therein day and night, that thou mayest observe to do according to all that is written therein: for then thou shalt make thy way prosperous, and then thou shalt have good success.

Proverbs 15:22

> Without deliberation, plans go wrong; but with many advisers, they succeed.

Proverbs 16:20

> He who has skill in a matter will succeed; he who trusts in Adonai will be happy.

Proverbs 17:8

> A bribe works like a charm, in the view of him who gives it — wherever it turns, it succeeds.

Proverbs 20:18

> After consultation, plans succeed; so take wise advice when waging war.

Proverbs 21:30

> No wisdom, discernment or counsel succeeds against Adonai.

Proverbs 28:13

> He who conceals his sins will not succeed; he who confesses and abandons them will gain mercy.

Please answer the following question:

- What does God measure success on?

Boland

VALUES
vs.
SUCCESS

My son, forget not my law.
Let thine heart keep my commandments.
For length of days, and long life, and peace,
shall they add to thee.
Let not mercy and truth forsake thee.
Bind them about thy neck, write them upon
the table of thine heart.
So shalt thou find favor and good
understanding in the sight of God and man.
Proverbs 3:1-4

Success based on a personal value system yields real results. What we value in life is what we hold as fundamental to our core belief system and cherish, honor, and consider important. These are things that are not up for debate or discussion. These are the things that make us who we are. These are the things that are the basis of why we take the actions, make the statements and live the life we do. Unfortunately, what we value is not shared by everyone we meet! As a matter of fact, not everyone who calls themselves a "Christian" holds to the same value system! We must, therefore, understand and not be shocked at that fact when dealing with someone else's idea of truth, morals, and honesty. Dr. Howie Hendricks, in his classic presentation concerning a "value system," attempts to clarify how each of us develops what they think, say and do.[xxix] It is within this structure, as he sets it out, how each of us establish our own set of rules for living and making all major decisions. He illustrates the ground rules of this by sharing a conversation between a father and daughter concerning the idea of values and what that really means. The girl's father broke it down into two distinct positions:

- Learning, what motivates people to gain knowledge
- Teaching, what stimulates people to reach out to others.

These so-called levels illustrate what influences individuals to do certain things, notice the stimulation/motivation graph. Each level explains the following:

Behavior

Success is based on behavior. So, why do we behave the way we do? What a person stands up for, puts up with, and approves speaks volumes of who they are and what they believe. Whether good, bad, or ugly. No one can say they believe one way and act another! So, what have you established as your value system is what you show to others, not the other way around. However, a person's conduct falls into three categories, explained, excused, or forgiven[xxx]

Explainable Behavior	Excusable Behavior
a) It is possible to see *why* it could happen. b) It was inevitable. c) It is still not right.	a) It *is* appropriate b) It is justifiable, based on the culture c) It is overlooked because we have been forgiven

Personal Disclosure

In seeking to understand ourselves and how we are motivated for success, we must then ask the following questions:

- How much do we really know about ourselves?
- What areas & subjects are not up for discussion?
- What areas & subjects can be discussed openly?
- How much do we know about the people around us?
- How much are we willing to open up to others?
- How much are others willing to open up to us?

WHAT WE THINK, SAY, & DO ☐

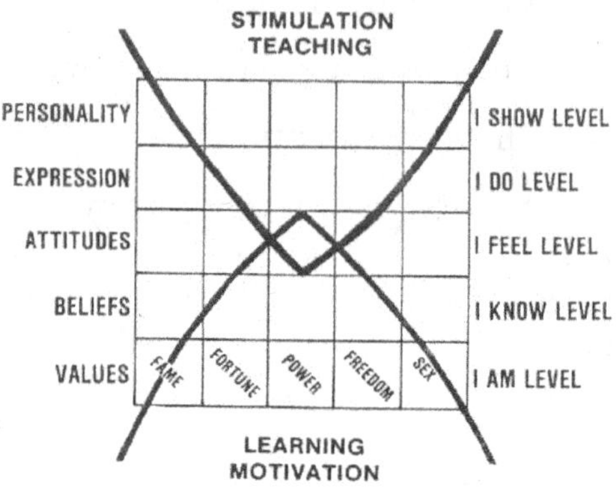

According to the graph, we only reach out to others at the level considered "performance." This would be from the **"I show"** to the **"I feel"** levels. We normally do not open ourselves up or allow anyone to understand us any deeper than this. The **"I know"** and **"I am"** levels are considered undebatable & untouchable because that contains our core convictions. It is here, each of us holds our deepest, strongest, most significant, and highly private opinions and motivations. We become vulnerable when we let others into these areas of our lives:

The "I Show" level (visible & observable)

This is what everyone knows and sees of each of us. This is what everyone sees first. Most people enter and understand our world by the way we act and behave around them, be it:

- Funny
- Irreverent
- Serious
- Social
- Athletic
- Studious

The "I Do" level (accomplish & express)

Others attempt to read into our position on various matters as we express ourselves by being:

- Active
- Motivated
- Assertive
- Inquisitive
- Approachable
- Defiant
- Successful

The "I Feel" level (opinions & attitudes)

Others attempt to interpret what we support or not so much by the terminology we use (which they hear), but by:

- Facial expressions we make,
- Other nonverbal ways in which we express ourselves.

The "I Know" level
(where values meet experience)

These last two areas are not up for debate, because this is where we have decided:

- What we accept as true.
- What we have confidence in.
- What we have faith in.
- What we are certain about.
- What we rely on.

In other words, I know what all these sources have told me, but it is here where I must decide for myself what I believe!

The "I Am" level
(where morals, ethics, & principles are established, held and cherished)

<u>Who am I?</u>

- It began at birth and will conclude at death.
- What one becomes, will change over the years based on everything stated here.
- Each person establishes their very private and personal basic level of who and what they are after a lifetime of being told:
  - What to do.
  - What to believe.
- One fact I have concluded is that no one can decide the values and beliefs of another person.
- It is here we decide and define success!

BIBLE STUDY

Mark 12:28-30 (ESV)
> Hear, O Israel, the Lord our God, the
> Lord is one. Love the Lord your God
> with all your heart and with all your
> soul and with all your mind and with
> all your strength.

Proverbs 19:1 (ESV)
> Better is a poor person who walks in
> his integrity than one who is crooked in
> speech and is a fool.

Luke 6:31 (ESV)
> And as you wish that others would do
> to you, do so to them.

Proverbs 12:22 (ESV)
> Lying lips are an abomination to the
> Lord, but those who act faithfully are
> his delight.

James 1:19-20 (ESV)
> Know this, my beloved brothers: let
> every person be quick to hear, slow to
> speak, slow to anger; for the anger of
> man does not produce the
> righteousness of God.

1 Timothy 5:8 (ESV)
> But if anyone does not provide for his
> relatives, and especially for members of
> his household, he has denied the faith
> and is worse than an unbeliever.

Proverbs 15:27 (ESV)
> Whoever is greedy for unjust gain
> troubles his own household, but he
> who hates bribes will live.

Matthew 16:26 (ESV)
> For what will it profit a man if he gains
> the whole world and forfeits his soul?
> Or what shall a man give in return for
> his soul?

Please answer the following questions:
- What do you think God values?
- Do these verses line up with your values?

Boland

Success

QUALIFYING SUCCESS

On receiving this message, David was pleased. There was something he could do for the king that would qualify him to be his son-in-law! He lost no time but went right out, he and his men, killed the hundred Philistines, brought their evidence back in a sack, and counted it out before the king, mission completed...
1 Samuel 18:26-27 (MSG)

What Qualifies As Success?

<u>Licensing</u>

In certain professions a license is a must, if not a requirement. Particularly, if an individual is ever to be considered a success. The requirements of licensing are based on testing, experience, and knowledge. Locally and nationally individuals benefit from people knowing that they are a licensed professional. Depending on their vocation, individuals are able to expand and build on what they consider to be their success into wider and broader areas because of the type license they have attained. This gives them increased visibility that brings within itself the potential of further success. Depending on the type of license, that document could enable an individual to expand globally without the added burden of tariffs, hassles, or the stress of building relationships with their chosen overseas business field.[xxxi]

Certification

Either fresh from high school or college, an individual can get further training and certifications either in their chosen career or profession. This is a great way to advance in the workplace. Certification increases an individual's chances of landing a job, the next job, or advancing at the current company. Taking the initiative to pursue certification shows an employer that an individual is self-motivated, credible, proactive, and committed to their future success.

Meeting Eligibility

Have you as an individual seeking success consider looking into the requirements of eligibility for positions above you? Have you considered asking what a person needs to accomplish in order to be promoted? Have you looked into the company timeline for moving up in the ranks? It is not a workplace sin. It is not a violation of ethics to ask questions even in the later interviews. I would not ask these questions in the early stages of the process. However, if you are the primary candidate or the new hire, it is not out of line to gently ask about what it takes to move up. That is after you make certain what it is your current job entails, requires, and is expected of you. Then you can ask questions of upward mobility.

Meeting Criteria

How is success measured? Success can be measure by a simple yes or no. Yes we did or no we did not do or achieve or goal. Success can even be a moving object such as an ongoing project that can be measured on a scale. Success doesn't need to be numerical, although breaking down objectives, projects, or workloads to numbers allows even the simplest of minds the ease of understanding. Tracking the work we do indicates how well something is or is not working. It allows the observer, donor, and/or manager to monitor progress. It allows standards to be set so those who need to know can tell how well these have been met. It marks clear progress through charts and graphs. This shows the trends that are clearly established. It identifies areas needing to be developed or those needing to be improved. It is crucial in decision making for evaluating, directing, policy formulating, and managing. It keeps individuals focused on what is important such as goal setting and action planning.[xxxii]

Passing Scrutiny

So you want to be a success, but not sure what you want to do. First question is what are your limitation? Before anything else, you'll need to make sure you have the required skills to complete whatever. Money? Knowledge base? Tools and equipment? Employees? All the above? Think you're going to have your hands full? I might add some others you might not have thought of for any job. Competent communication skills, leadership, negotiating ability, and conflict management. If you are going into the workplace and want to succeed you will need these, guaranteed! Whether you are just starting out or in the middle of life there are certain things you need to consider to succeed. So, what is it we need to know to be successful?

- Who do we need to know?
  - The chain of command, assignments for oversight, specifics of job assignment, details of projects, documentation, and completion.
- What do we need to know?
  - Due dates, what order, will there be flexibility, and potential plan B.
- Why do we need to know this stuff?
  - There are certain things your job depends on.
  - Do not be afraid to ask questions.
- How soon do we need to know this stuff?
  - Be proactive in reviewing your area of responsibility.

Once these questions are answered, it'll be easy to find success within any workplace environment.[xxxiii]

Restrictions

What would limit someone from being successful in life, at work, or with family? Being dishonest, untruthful, or immoral? Not being in the moment with those around you, such as creative, sensitive, or concerned? Not caring to improve oneself or others? Not willing to learn something new or seek to learn something not known?

It is a fact that if we yield to our failures they will control and limit future achievements. Greed over gratitude will restrict promotions, relationships and workplace conditions. Being negative or surrounding yourself with those who project negativity will limit any positive possibilities in life, relationships, or work. Life is hard but by allowing the negative things in life to break us, knock us down, or keep us from reaching our greatest potential is not an option. Lecturer Chatri Sityodtong recommends that everyone strive to learn, grow, and evolve every day. [xxxiv]

Again I ask, what qualifies as a success? How does one know they achieved success? Is it having acquired a license, or certificate? Is it becoming eligible for something? Is it meeting a certain criteria? Could it be just meeting the requirements of a specific job or title? What limits or ceilings are there to achieving success? Are these real disadvantages and boundaries self-made or based on some society rules?

Those wishing to go into business for themselves focus on the potential for getting licensing to do something! The license may be local, state, or federal based on the type business one pursues. The government side is more about control and taxing income than providing a roadmap to success. Individuals and corporations understand this is an evil necessity on the road to prosperity, profit, and wealth.

Certificates have become increasingly popular among a generation of people who seek quick completion to programs that lead to specific jobs. They want instant results which lead to what they see as their idea of success. Certificates include everything from cosmetology, welding to nursing.

Another qualifier toward success includes the idea of being rewarded for goals attained. Belief in a reward system based on a particular goal must have importance, meaning, and be compelling for someone to pursue it. The individual must have an inner belief that the goal is achievable and that the reward is worthwhile. There must be the belief that the plans laid out are attainable.

To be successful one must establish a criteria in order to measure the road to success. Goals must be trackable so they can indicate how well something is working or not. If we know what we are shooting for then we can set standards. These standards will indicate how well they are meeting goals. It is by establishing the goals, setting the standards, and measuring the progress that we evaluate performance and measure success.[xxxv]

What is the idea of putting limits on success? These limits include the amount of time, energy and effort someone decides to put into their work. The more time spent on an assignment the more possibility of a loss of motivation. Maybe they do not have sufficient information and loose interest. Maybe they are surrounded by inadequate advisors. Family time must be the first consideration in limiting any workload. Then there is personal play time. How about the work environment whether it is good, bad, or indifferent. There is a direct correlation between a person's indifference to their work environment and the effort and time they put into it. A strong limitation is the idea of personal income vs. personal expenditures. This area causes many individuals to restrict their choices of jobs, assignments, and work locations. Other restrictions include personal motivation, work ethic, creativity, culture, and optimism. What about the cost of obtaining your goal? Let's say white collar vs. blue collar jobs. On-the-job Training vs. Trade School vs. Community

College vs. University? Paying for college vs. student loans? Is the idea of paying for college as you go worth the effort? Certainly, there will not be a heavy debt at the end of the experience? Student loans will get you the goal faster and one can concentrate on the course more but the long-term effects are stressful and burdensome.

BIBLE STUDY

Colossians 3:23 (ESV)
> Whatever you do, work heartily, as for the Lord and not for men,

Proverbs 16:3 (ESV)
> Commit your work to the Lord, and your plans will be established.

Proverbs 14:23 (ESV)
> In all toil there is profit, but mere talk tends only to poverty.

Proverbs 22:29 (ESV)
> Do you see a man skillful in his work? He will stand before kings; he will not stand before obscure men.

Please answer the following questions:
Based on these verses:

- What do these verses say qualifies as a success?
- How does one know they achieved success?

Success

TOOLS OF SUCCESS

The tools of our trade aren't for marketing or manipulation, but they are for demolishing that entire massively corrupt culture. We use our powerful God-tools for smashing warped philosophies, tearing down barriers erected against the truth of God, fitting every loose thought and emotion and impulse into the structure of life shaped by Christ.
Our tools are ready at hand for clearing the ground of every obstruction and building lives of obedience into maturity.
2 Corinthians 10:4-6 (MSG)

Education

One's knowledge base doesn't necessarily end when you graduate. In fact, it has never been easier to acquire knowledge. It has been understood that getting knowledge specific to your workplace will eventually yield benefits. The skills one has developed over the years can translate into knowledge that is considered an asset to both an individual and a company. Skills acquired at one workplace transfer to other job opportunities.

Warren Buffett[xxxvi]

Resources

To the secular world success is a means to an end for any of the following:

- It is freedom;
- It is happiness;
- It is taking risk;
- It is an attitude;
- It is impacting life;
- It is helping others;
- It is about integrity;
- It is a state of mind;
- It is all about money;
- It is the unachievable;
- It is having inner peace;
- It is about achievement;
- it is overcoming obstacles;

- It is about achieving goals;
- It is all about being selfish;
- It is about business growth;
- It is being able to support family;
- It is a journey rather than a goal;
- It is about getting others to do the work;
- It is about building a business to sell at a profit;
- It is about personal respect at home, community, and business;
- It is about leaving the world a little bit better off;
- It is being authenticity, having passion, and a sense of wonder;
- It is being engaged, challenged, and growing;
- It is owning a bigger piece of the global business pie. [xxxvii]

<u>Resolve</u>

The first thing is that you must have a burning desire to succeed. You must have established your goals for being a success before it will become a reality. You must have a desire, that strong feeling or intense longing to do something. But be warned though: desire is no substitute for hard work. What is needed next is the inner drive to succeed. This is the effort it takes to achieve something. It is the will power that will decide the consequence of your actions be they good, bad, or useless. You can have the best of intentions, but without discipline one cannot achieve anything. Without discipline, disorder is king, plans are misunderstood, nothing is achieved and outsiders only see chaos and confusion.[xxxviii] It's hard to remember in the middle of the battle that you are not alone. It helps to take a step back once in a while. It helps to know that others have been in situations just like you and seek their help, guidance, and assistance.

<u>Problems</u>

Is there really a purpose for pain and suffering during failure? These twins of misery have been around since the introduction of sin![xxxix] Jesus suffering was for the forgiveness of sin![xl] Facing our personal short comings the suffering gives rise to an opportunity to experience the peace that passes all understanding. Handled appropriately, failure can bring about glory and honor to God by our conduct and character. Our other option is to simply allow our situation and individual affliction to become personal torment without value. Which of these do you think will be viewed by those around us as making a positive difference? The difference comes down to whether we respond or react to the situation? Whether we respond and recover thus succeeding through failure or react and further sink into the mire of failure!

There are several ways to look at the suffering which follows failure. The secular world says you can quit and therefore run away. The other option is to allow the conditions to happen and be resilient thereby accepting the experience of discomfort while keeping sight of the end goal. If we simply react to the problems of life, we set ourselves up for compounding and multiplying our problems.

Scripture tells us to be careful: we could be persuaded to seek things other than God. This could send us into a trajectory of sin and death and compound the original failure we faced. This road ultimately leads to eternal separation from all things good, honorable, and godly. Under such influence, the desire for success can grip our life.[xli] Then, we find ourselves continually attracted toward supporting unwise decisions and questionable causes.[xlii] This will further lead us away from godly pursuits[xliii], and eventually take us completely away from God and our goal of real success.[xliv] By always reacting to the issues of life rather than facing up to them, we open the door to other problems.

What might those other issues be? We might begin to deal with the idea of worshipping material things. We might focus on conditions or things that never satisfy. We might end up in a death spiral of being enchanted by unexplainable lifestyles. We might overreact by hating and blaming others for our failure(s) for no apparent reason. We might take on a violent behavior. We might even have an unhealthy possessiveness of people or things. We might develop a reputation for having regular outbursts of anger. We might become driven by selfish and unhealthy desires. We might just become rebellious and irreverent toward things of God, family, and anything considered "good and acceptable".[xlv] This attitude and way of life even carries over to finding fault in others, combined with the inability to accept one's own shortcomings.[xlvi] Over time, this routine leads to an attitude of hopelessness[xlvii], uncontrolled greed, and disillusionment with everything good a distrust of everyone who even tries to help.[xlviii] One sad side note is that our current culture accepts these snowflakes as victims of their circumstances and consider it as a winning attitude! However, it will sometimes drive a person to fighting serious bouts of depression[xlix]. Check out the downhill slide and final days of King Saul! Read about him in detail in 1 Samuel.[l] One the other hand, King David had his moments of depression but took it to God and was honest with his feelings and confessed his sin and failure. (Read Psalms)

There is hope. Only if we respond to these issues by seeking a higher purpose and a better outcome for our life. One way is to set your mind on God's Word when in the middle of your mess.[li] Another is to pray about your situation or condition. Then put feet to your prayers as you can and have opportunity. This means seeking forgiveness, making restitution, etc. After that, leave each situation to the Lord without constantly worrying about it. Worry is defined as assuming responsibilities God never intended us to have.[lii] Give God thanks because thankfulness should inhabit ones' prayer life[liii] and give Him glory & praise in everything (good/bad times, failures, trials, tribulations, crisis, illnesses, accidents, etc.). As stated earlier, believers know these situations develop Christian character resulting in a lifestyle of hope. We also know that true godly optimism does not disappoint.[liv] Finally, in responding to whatever life throws at us (failures, pain, insults, disappointments, problems) we develop godly conduct, character, and trust in God because we know He is trustworthy.[lv]

Planning

It is a fact that success does not just drop out of the sky! First of all, one must have all the necessary skills to meet the goals one dreamt about. If you aren't the one with the necessary skills you must hire those with these skills and talents in order to make the dream come true. However, at that point you are dependent on those who possess the skilled labor! Making a list of all the skills, talents, licenses and certifications essential and mandatory is a crucial step in the planning process. These skills could include anything from building trades, communications, IT, leadership competency, and conflict management. Word of warning: God's Word is clear that believers are not to be tied in marriage or business with unbelievers.[lvi]

The next step in planning is to understand the scale of the project the person or group is trying to take on! Many plans fail due to someone not realizing they don't have the funding, work power, skills, or necessary materials to complete the dream. Understanding the full extent of the project has to happen early in the planning process. One recommendation is to obtain several viewpoints from different people who understand the information needed to meet the end results. Miscalculating the smallest of information can cause misalignments, missed assignments, even missed dates which could all result in delays and pushback, or ultimately the failure or collapse of the whole project or mission.

Most dreams come to fruition after what I will call the core team mastering the basics of the learning curve. It may sound simple, but the basics are the core components holding the project together. This is the who, what, when, why, and how. These questions have to be asked and answered in order for a smooth transition towards success to occur. The basic include such things as risk assessments and a plan B, C, and maybe a D too. There needs to be timelines and they need to be verified, set, and approved (yet flexible). There needs to be clear and defined priorities. There needs to be closely accurate "estimated" costs. There needs to be clear procedures that are agreed to by all parties. Finally, there needs to be methods of reporting and a chain of command that all agree upon.

Another area that need clarification is assigned tasks for all team members. This includes deciding who is accountable for every aspect of every part of the project. This helps to rule out uncertainty. It is vital that the cost of the project are clear because this reduces time or money lost when the work commences. Another area of clarification is the reporting methods and timeframes. Determining deadlines and establish baselines as reference points to measure the project or mission's success are crucial.

Now just because a plan is in place doesn't mean it shouldn't be reviewed regularly. Every plan should be proactively tracked for accuracy, relevance, and brought up to date. Plans must also undergo several reviews before any project or mission is completed. To be reviewed appropriately there should be updates from relevant areas and individuals within the workforce concerning cost, time management, ratio of completion, and milestones met. Discussing this information with the team and comparing it to the plan will helps assess whether the project is progressing as expected. When reviewing the plan, obstacles, and known and unknown risks need to be considered. When comparing pre-anticipated risks or delays to obvious ones there should already be a "plan B" in place. The more one can plan to prevent and manage problems, the better.

So, the project completion is in sight! How should one plan for closure? Step one, make sure everyone is clear on what's required in order to ensure the project is complete and on time. Step two, keep everyone up to date on the process all along the way. This ensures no small steps are missed and everyone is able to complete their tasks on time within budget. Upon completion, a concluding briefing is advised. It should communicate all the last-minute information sourced throughout the lifecycle of the project or mission to all members involved. To some this may seem like an overkill but all these steps are vital to ensuring that anything undertaken is a success. After all, the more painstakingly put together a plan is, the more likely it'll be to achieve success with minimal delays and stress.[lvii]

Time management

One British survey found that 82% of people don't have any kind of time management system to speak of.[lviii] The practice of time management requires concentration and awareness in planning in order to control a busy day and attain goals. What helps is prioritization, goal setting, and appropriately organizing one's mind including the space around them. This is the only way to overcome barriers which interfere with productive use of time. Discovering your personal productivity rhythm is another area. Are you a morning or night person? This effects how a person maximizes their daily work. This approach involves arranging similar tasks, organizing them and working them up together for minimum interruptions. The survey found that the most productive individuals are those who are well-balanced. This means balance in between their work, personal, and family demands. This does not mean each should have an equal balance of time but rather prioritizing what is important at a particular time. Work should be dedicated to what is essential for career. Home should be dedicated to family and/or personal. To be most productive, you need to establish a positive working environment that is conducive to getting your work done. This means eliminating any external workplace distractions that promote procrastination.

Expert Advice

Seeking to be mentored by those who have been there and done that is advisable and encouraged. Those who have been there and done that, know what to do. They know how to do what they are experts in doing. They learned what it takes to speed up the learning process to complete a tasks and complete them more proficiently. Those who have been there and done that, have a wealth of experience to offer. They have a unique point of view on how to get things accomplished efficiently. They normally anticipate future trends before others even recognize that change is about to occur. Those who have been there and done that, are experts in their field. Some of them may not know everything but they know more than those just starting out and this is why they are so valuable. Those who have been there and done that, know what works and what doesn't work. They have learned through mistakes, failures, and successes what works and doesn't work and can help generate better ideas. They can sort out the good from the bad.

Those who have been there and done that, have a vast network of people they know. The can get things done that others just starting out cannot. They can break down the challenge of growing a working network whether organically or through cold connecting. They can assist those just starting out by giving endorsements. Those who have been there and done that, can give those just starting out the exposure necessary to succeed. Their endorsement and encouragement can legitimize someone just starting out in a workplace or mission. Unfortunately, there are some who are too proud to admit they need to be mentored. They are too proud to enter the process. Such conduct and action can be harmful to their potential growth personally, professionally, and Spiritually.[lix]

Computer Competency

In today's world in order to be a success any individual must have competent computer skills. Computer skills consist of both hardware and software. Employers have come to expect employees to have competent computer skills which go beyond twitter, Facebook, snapchat and the like. More generally speaking one should have a general working knowledge of the following: Microsoft Office, Excel, and PowerPoint. Social Media, Email & Information Management, Data Entry, Digital Calendars (Google, Outlook, etc.), File Sharing Programs (Dropbox, Google Drive, etc.), Workplace Chat (Slack, Microsoft Teams, etc.), Video Conferencing, Cloud Backup Software (Dropbox Pro, Carbonite, etc.), and Project Management Software (Asana, Jira, etc.) When listing computer skills in a resume one must be specific. The resume must include examples of computer skills which will add to the company. The cover letter must address any computer related skills that were mentioned in the advertisement and how an individual's skill sets met those needs.[lx]   Be aware that employers do check for social media post before and after hiring individuals that are not in-line with company values.

Boland

BIBLE STUDY

Ephesians 5:15-17
> See then that ye walk circumspectly, not as fools, but as wise, Redeeming the time, because the days are evil. Wherefore be ye not unwise but understanding what the will of the Lord is.

Proverbs 27:17
> Iron sharpens iron; so a man sharpens the countenance of his friend.

Luke 14:28
> For which of you, intending to build a tower, sits not down first, and counts the cost, whether he have sufficient to finish it?

Please answer the following questions:
- What can you tell is needed for success from the previous verses?
- What is missing from these verses?

Boland

Success

BEYOND SUCCESS

*Really! There's no such thing as self-rescue,
pulling yourself up by your bootstraps.
The cost of rescue is beyond our means,
and even then it doesn't guarantee
Life forever,
or insurance against the Black Hole.*
Psalm 49:7-9 (MSG)

So, you have accomplished much. You have been recognized by your peers. You have plaques on your wall. Now what? Have you recognized yourself? Who you are is made up of the total of those experiences that made you. These are what shaped you into that success the large, the small, and the insignificant decisions.[lxi] You can't always control the outcomes of those decisions because they come with consequences good, bad and indifferent. You can, however, control choices you make. God promises to give us choices.[lxii] So, shouldn't every one of the decisions a person makes consider their relationship to God and their personal pursuit of success? What most us fail to consider is that in pursuing ambitious targets such as success we have peer pressure that comes along with that and takes its toll.

All this pressure and stress takes its toll on the body and brain. This constant strain makes it almost impossible to ignore and eventually affects job performance in the workplace.

It is a fact that we live in a world of instant gratification and deadlines that always seem to be due yesterday. It seems easy to allow our workload to pile up until it becomes too much. While the work pace appears normal at first, over the years it leads to a condition called "burnout." The idea of burnout is a state of mind seen as normal working conditions that affect the physical and mental well-being of an employee.

Signs of burnout include but are not limited to the following: anxiety, sleeplessness, change in attitude in the work environment, change in relationships, employee turnover, lower productivity, and poor morale.

The careers and professions most likely to be affected and experience this condition are jobs that have monotonous work environments; jobs that create imbalance between work and personal life; jobs that require significant overtime; jobs that have little influence over decisions that affect working conditions; jobs that are isolated; jobs with strained work relationships.

Professions that have been found with the most burnout conditions are physicians, emergency workers, teachers, care givers, and prison guards to name a few. [lxiii]

The mental signs of burnout include dreading work, lacking interest or motivation for things in general, decreased sense of accomplishment, uncontrollable procrastination, the feeling of being incapable of coping with new challenges. The signs of physical burnout include general state of exhaustion, chronic stress, changes into poor sleep habits, sudden & frequent health problems, ranging from headaches and colds to mental health illnesses like depression and anxiety. The signs of emotional burnout include cynicism at work (assuming you were not cynical to begin with), irritability or anger at work, sudden and intense dislike for your job, feelings of hopelessness at work, the need for isolation from others. [lxiv]

Personal Window

The only way that I have found to successfully counter burnout is to seek true peace of mind in Scripture.[lxv] It is to face whatever is troubling us through dealing with it, not out of fear, but by the strength of God in prayer. Also, by the help of friends and family and the Word of God.[lxvi] I know that the stress of the moment and the pain within is genuine. I know that as we go through these conditions it seems to be endless. However, if you are a believer in Christ, know that the unbelieving world is watching your every action, move, and word. They want to see what you will do in that same situation that they have found, did find, or will find themselves in one day. They don't want to know what your precious scripture has to say. They want to see how your faith helps you through real life situations. [lxvii]

Success

Bible Study

Matthew 6:30-33 (MSG)

> If God gives such attention to the appearance of wildflowers (most of which are never even seen) don't you think he'll attend to you, take pride in you, do his best for you? What I'm trying to do here is to get you to relax, to not be so preoccupied with getting, so you can respond to God's giving. People who don't know God and the way he works fuss over these things, but you know both God and how he works. Steep your life in God-reality, God-initiative, God-provisions. Don't worry about missing out. You'll find all your everyday human concerns will be met.

Matthew 11:28-30 (MSG)

> Are you tired? Worn out? Burned out on religion? Come to me. Get away with me and you'll recover your life. I'll show you how to take a real rest. Walk with

me and work with me, watch how I do it. Learn the unforced rhythms of grace. I won't lay anything heavy or ill-fitting on you. Keep company with me and you'll learn to live freely and lightly.

Please answer the following questions:
- What do the scriptures say about dealing with burnout?

Boland

CONCLUSION

Whoso hath this world's good, and
sees his brother have need, and
shuts up his bowels of compassion from him,
how dwelleth the love of God in him?

1 John 3:17

Just as in the days of the Laodiceans, our world views success with eyes towards materialism, monetary gain, and the accumulation of earthly goods.[lxviii] Even inside the church the very idea of health and wealth is a secular world view and has no place in there. Those deceitful teachers and preachers who spew this false gospel know this. Yet, they continue to do so because it is profitable for them personally. From the very beginning of creation God's idea of success is humans having a relationship with Him and each other. Throughout the scriptures having a positive relationship with God was seen as an unquestionable advantage against one's enemies, in dealing with life's issues, and from being viewed as being blessed. When Jesus appeared on earth, God reestablished His priority of having a relationship with Him and that mattered more than material success. Having a relationship with God through Jesus Christ is more important than any earthly gain. Living one's life centered around a core value system based on scriptural integrity, honesty, morality, and dignity leads to success beyond our wildest imagination. Such character, conduct, and decorum opens doors of opportunity most people only dream about. The pursuit of such behavior, manner, and actions will always lead to a positive outcome. To continually look for the good in others can only be considered successful and beneficial for the individual, professional, and family life in the long run.[lxix]

Bible Study

Revelation 15-17 (MSG)
> I know you inside and out and find little to my liking. You're not cold, you're not hot—far better to be either cold or hot! You're stale. You're stagnant. You make me want to vomit. You brag, 'I'm rich, I've got it made, I need nothing from anyone,' oblivious that in fact you're a pitiful, blind beggar, threadbare and homeless.

Revelation 3:20-21 (CJB)
> Here, I'm standing at the door, knocking. If someone hears my voice and opens the door, I will come into him and eat with him, and he will eat with me. I will let him who wins the victory sit with me on my throne, just as I myself also won the victory and sat down with my Father on his throne.

Please answer the following questions:
- What are these verses saying in reference to success overall?
- What are these verses saying in reference to God's idea of success?

Boland

Success

BIBLIOGRAPHY

WHAT IS SUCCESS

[i]

What Does Success Mean? By Lyn Christian, SoulSalt Inc. (2019) https://soulsalt.com/what-does-success-mean/

[ii]

Joshua 1:8

[iii]

Henry, Matthew. "Complete Commentary on Joshua 1". "Henry's Complete Commentary on the Whole Bible". https://www.studylight.org/commentaries/eng/mhm/joshua-1.html. 1706.

FAILURE vs. SUCCESS

[iv]

American Heritage® Dictionary of the English Language, Third Edition. Houghton Mifflin Harcourt Publishing Company (1993)

[v]

"Qualitative." Merriam-Webster.com Dictionary, Merriam-Webster, https://www.merriam-webster.com/dictionary/qualitative. Accessed 23 Mar. 2022.

MEASURING SUCCESS

[vi]

7 Ways to Measure True Success, Success metrics are changing every day. By Chirag Kulkarni, Co-founder and CEO https://www.inc.com/chirag-kulkarni/7-ways-to-measure-true-success.html

[vii] *Principles of Successful Business from Proverbs* by Greg Koukl, Stand to Reason, Published on 06/24/2013 https://www.str.org/w/principles-of-successful-business-from-proverbs

[viii]

Proverbs   3:5–7 16:3 22:1

[ix]

Proverbs 19:15, 22:13, 10:26,30:15

x

Proverbs 13:11b, 18:19, 12:11, 28:19, 21:25–26, 27:18, 20:13, 6:9–11, 24:33–34

xi

Proverbs 12:24, 12:27, 10:4

xii

Proverbs 11:1,20:23,16:11,20:10

xiii

Proverbs 10:2a, 13:11a, 15:27a,19:22b, 20:17, 21:6, 28:16b

xiv

Proverbs 21:5, 16:9, 21:31

xv

Proverbs 6:6–8, 30:25, 20:4

xvi

Proverbs 24:27, 27:23–24a, 30:27

xvii

Proverbs17:18

xviii

Proverbs 24:4

xix

Proverbs 30:8–9,19:4, 7,14:20, 10:15, 11:28, 18:11, 23:4–5,18:23

xx

Proverbs 3:9–10, 11:25, 19:17, 11:24a, 19:16

xxi

Proverbs 15:22, 20:18,11:14,24:6

xxii

Proverbs 10:5, 14:23, 26:15,19:24

xxiii

Proverbs 11:24, 22:7, 22:16,22:29

xxiv

Ecclesiastes 3:22

ASSESSING SUCCESS

xxv

Wooden: A Lifetime of Observations and Reflections On and

Off the Court, by John Wooden, McGraw-Hill, (1997)
xxvi

https://www.linkedin.com/company/success-systems/
xxvii

Success Mindsets: Your Keys to Unlocking Greater Success in Your Life, Work, & Leadership by Ryan Gottfredson, Morgan James Publishing (2020)
xxviii

The Only Definition of Success That Matters, By Jeff Haden, Contributing editor, Inc.

VALUES vs. SUCCESS

xxix

Teaching to Change Lives: Seven Proven Ways to Make Your Teaching Come Alive, by Howard Hendricks, Multnomah, (2003)
xxx

Dr. Steve Armstrong, LeTourneau University,
    Bible studies for Life, "Overcome Temptation",
    http://www.biblestudiesbysteve.com/SundaySchool/
    archive_of_bible_studies.htm

QUALIFYING SUCCESS

xxxi

What to Consider Before Licensing Your Brand, By: Dawn Allcot, Contributor, U.S. Chamber of Commerce
https://www.uschamber.com/co/start/strategy/brand-licensing-pros-and-cons
xxxii

https://www.usj.edu.mo/wp-content/uploads/2018/12/Success-criteria.pdf
xxxiii

The Importance of Planning to Achieve Success, by Sebastian Bos, experteer.com
https://us.experteer.com/magazine/planning-to-achieve-success/
xxxiv

10 Essential Rules For Success In Life, by Chatri Sityodtong

https://chatrisityodtong.com/blog/life/10-essential-rules-for-success-in-life/
xxxv

Success Mindsets: Your Keys to Unlocking Greater Success in Your Life, Work, & Leadership, by Ryan Gottfredson, Morgan James Publishing (2020)
TOOLS OF SUCCESS

xxxvi

102 Warren Buffett Quotes on Investing, Life & More | Rule #1 Investing, by Phil Town, Rule One Investing publications, https://www.ruleoneinvesting.com/blog/how-to-invest/warren-buffett-quotes-on-investing-success/
xxxvii

62 Business Leaders Answer: What Does Success Mean To You?, Startup Advice, by Matt Wilson / May 25, 2022 https://www.under30ceo.com/62-business-leaders-answer-what-does-success-mean-to-you/
xxxviii

Tools of Success: Desire, Drive and Discipline
By Abundant Robert K. Awolugutu 2022 Modern Ghana
xxxix

Romans 5:12, 20
xl

Hebrews 2:8-11; 1 Peter 3:18
xli

2 Samuel 11:2-4
xlii

Matthew 5:28
xliii

1 John 2:16
xliv

Romans 6:12, 23
xlv

Galatians 5:20
xlvi

Genesis 2:12

---

xlvii

Proverbs 15:13

xlviii

Proverbs 15:16-17, 16:8

xlix

Exodus 6:9

l

1 Samuel 16 – 28.

li

Psalm 1:2-3

lii

Philippians 4:6-7

liii

1 Thessalonians 5:18

liv

Romans 5:3-5

lv

2 Peter 3:11; 2 Corinthians 1:9

lvi

2 Corinthians 6:14

lvii

The Importance of Planning to Achieve Success by Sebastian Bos, Experteer GmbH (2022) https://us.experteer.com/magazine/planning-to-achieve-success/

lviii

Time Management Statistics & Facts (New 2021 Research) by Ben Richardson (2021) https://development-academy.co.uk/news-tips/time-management-statistics-2021-research/

lix

9 Reasons It's Important To Work With Experts, by Davis Tucker, 60 Second Marteter (2020) https://60secondmarketer.com/2020/10/20/9-reasons-its-important-to-work-with-experts/

lx

Important Computer Skills for Workplace Success, By Alison

Doyle, Balance Careers, Dotdash Meredith publishing (2020)
https://www.thebalancecareers.com/computer-skills-list-2063738
https://www.zippia.com/advice/computer-skills/

BEYOND SUCCESS

lxi

https://www.beyondteal.com/blog/what-happens-when-you-get-what-you-want-or-success-beyond-success
What Happens When You Get What You Want? Or Success Beyond Success! by Bruce Peters

lxii

Joshua 24:15, Galatians 5:13, 1 Peter 2:16, John 8:36

lxiii

Burnout Is Real: Signs of Chronic Workplace Stress (2019)
The Talkiatry branded Psychiatry practice is independently owned and operated by a licensed Psychiatrist. For more information about the relationship click here. ©2022 Talkiatry Management Services, LLC. All Rights Reserved.

lxiv

What Is Burnout Syndrome? Home Lifestyle Wellness
By Amie, Facty Staff (2019)
https://facty.com/lifestyle/wellness/what-is-burnout-syndrome/?style=quick&utm_source=adwords&adid=451422 789552&ad_group_id=82135430846&utm_medium=c-search&utm_term=burnout%20syndrome&utm_campaign=F H-USA-Search-What-Is-Burnout-Syndrome-Desktop&gclid=EAlalQobChMI7OqM-fXi-QIVrxPUAR3J-AMbEAAYAyAAEgla-vD_BwE

Burnout: 20 signs, causes, and how to prevent it
Julia Martins, (2022)
https://asana.com/resources/what-is-burnout?utm_campaign=NB--NAMER--EN--Catch-All--All-Device--DSA&utm_source=google&utm_medium=pd_cpc_nb&gclid=E AlalQobChMI7OqM-fXi-QIVrxPUAR3J-

---

AMbEAAYASAAEgJNGvD_BwE&gclsrc=aw.ds

lxv

John 14:27

lxvi

Isaiah 41:10; Proverbs 3:5-6; Psalm 23:4

lxvii

Peter 1:6-7, Isaiah 40:30-31, Romans 5:3-4, Joshua 1:9, Psalm 46:1

CONCLUSION

lxviii

Revelation 3:14-22

lxix

Deuteronomy 28:1-15

www.ingramcontent.com/pod-product-compliance
Lightning Source LLC
Chambersburg PA
CBHW052050150726

48002CB00002B/831